WHEN FUN IS NOT FUN

Let's go mum
Let's go play
Let's go have fun
My favourite place today

We arrive excitement ensues
Water park fun great news
Then the children laugh and stare
Call him names unaware

Shut down begins
The confusion sets in
The wall goes up
Won't let me in

Then home we trot
Doesn't seem to care a jot
Yes frustration builds
Quietness and still

On the bus
Questions are asked
Bully's why do they
Why why must they

Try and explain
Try to understand his pain
I experience it daily
But in reality

A child is a child
Innocent and mild
The adults guide
Words to Beguile

All he wanted was to have fun
But other children thought
Let's have some fun
Laugh and stare at someone

My lil boy does not understand
His confusion and pain
At others making fun
He has done nothing wrong

Approach the house
Windows mum not messy
People see in
Don't want to let them in

The next barriers bamboo
A neighbours garden
Yes it's true
Confusion sets in

His favourite friend
Bamboo
I can't see you
What did I do

It may be innocent
But his heart
Withdraws further in
What a day it's been

Into the home
Hurt and pain
Don't know what to do
What am I to do

Bed time it is
Stories to be read
Then slowly says
No water park again

Can we go somewhere else
No water park but climb yes
Ask him why,
Don't want to be wet

Why society does cruelty reign
Children so young
Bullying begins
What's the world done wrong

Children learn, model behave
It's so wrong and depraved
Teach my son I do
Bullying is cruel

Teach him no one less or more
That pride is before a fall
He asks why a bully is a coward
I tell him they hurt and what's more

To hurt another
In word or deed
To feel better
Is wrong indeed

I teach him walk away
It's better that way
What's done to one
Karma will repay

I say times three
He says times seven
Arc angels look down from heaven
With love for thee

Another hurts with words and deeds
Society when will you learn
A heart is soft and pliable
Your cruelty is despicable

Inclusion is an Illusion
When bullying is a solution
Isolation and stereotyping
Labelling equals discriminating

What is the solution
Conformity a pollution
Acceptance an illusion
Exclusion societies resolution

Stand we will Against bullying
Subtle and blatant it's all the same
No more crying
No more a game

Children deserve better than this
The cycle of division
There's a better solution
Let's start a revolution

Let's see the child
Not the difference
Label not the child
Celebrate difference

Written for all those who understand, have gone through, are going through the atrocities of

<u>AUTHORITY ABUSE S47</u>

We don't care
We will strip you bare
Rob you of those you love
It's our job

We come we visit
Isolate and investigate
Assess and twist
All we get

We don't care
The agenda is there
You asked for support
Now you will lose the lot

Accusations we create
Proof fabricate
Tear your family apart
Just to start

You dare ask for support
Now you will lose the lot
Save money
That's our job

Rip families apart
Break hearts
We don't give a jot
money we get is our lot

We will lie
Fabricate
We don't care if you cry
Will put you back in your crate

Don't dare ask for support
Don't dare point out
The laws we broke
Now you we will choke

Destroy your family
Destroy your heart
Destroy your mind
Don't care if we do

Stupid fool
You asked for support
Now we are coming for you
No one to protect you

No advocacy service
Everyone in our pocket
Cover each other's mistake
Drive into your heart a stake

Yes destroy your family we will
And enjoy it we will
Against your will
Swallow the poisonous pill

Ask for support
You stupid fool
Who can defend you
We have the money not you

Yes power we have
Abuse it we will
We never stop still
Destroy families we will

Why you ask
It simple don't you see
A budget we have
It more important than thee

We broke the law
Statutory guidelines too
You caught us out
So silence you we will

Threaten you
Scare you
Silence you
Stupid fool

You stupid fool
Money is our tool
To abuse you
That's what we will do

oh and while we are at it
There's another racket
Make money
It's worth a packet

Sell children for a fee
Tell lies to the adoptee
That's our job don't you see
To destroy your family

Bonuses we will get
For every child we steal
By the very lies we reveal
We have hard hearts of steel

You asked for support
Now you will get nowt
And worse than that
Loose the world that's what

No one cares
No one will defend
No one will protect
That will be the end

So many treated this way
Money the agenda
But all turn the heads away
As families are brought asunder.

No one will fight their corner
Will sit back and wonder
But not really ponder
Or challenge those in power

To all the parents who face the reality, I see your pain, I see you win, I see the falls, I see the pitfalls, stay strong, be proud, your not alone, many parents are with you, blessings to you all.

STOLEN TIME

We begin the journey
This is the reality
We see the difficulties
So we ask for an EHC

Forms to fill in
Pointless and Grimm
Refused point blank
Next mediation no thanks

Here we go
As promises broken
Mediation
Was not the solution

Here we go
More forms
Ask for an EHC
Well let's see

Oh my what a surprise
Yes this time
Assessments begin
And the blame game

Family law broken
Statutory guidelines breached
Lies and deceit
Paper trail is protection

Protection we need
As support we seek
Whilst they target the meek
To protect the budget this week

Forms upon forms,
Appeal upon appeal
Ready for judicial review
Many parents take this view

Time stolen from the children we love
As we become their targets
for fighting for what's needed
To allow our children the freedom

The freedom to learn
The freedom to be
The freedom to excel
To be the best they can be

Local authorities
Budgets to keep
Make many parents weep
With such absurdities

Ask for support
We care not a jot
But we will put you back in the box
That will be your lot

Don't think I joke
Ask many a folk
The parents accused
And bullied too

By local authorities
Yes that's true
Budgets, money
That's their reality

Parents who start this journey
Naive to begin
Hope for support
Hope to win

Those with the power
Abuse that power
Abuse the law
Think above the law

Parents accused
Threatened, bullied
to back off
But many do not.

So up the anti they do
They don't care about you
The budget is the priority
Parents the minority

When will someone not realise
The injustice families in crisis
No support is given
No statutory plan is given

Abuse of power still is
Prevalent, Insatiable, unshakable
Destroying families and lives
All for the sake of the budget

So many families torn apart
By the stress and pain
Of trying to win
The basic rights of an education

Society buries its head in the sand
Unaware of the greater plan
Local authorities have
In denying an EHC plan

So many families fighting each day
Staving off the callous attacks
Whilst caring for those they love
Whilst their Family is torn apart

Then here is the injustice
For the parents there is no justice
No one stands up for their rights
Unless charities join in the fight

Covert attacks made secret
Discredit, manipulate their failing system
To save money by hook or crook
They don't care they don't follow the book

Laws upon laws
Guidelines upon guidelines
Supposed to protect
But they use to discredit

Loop holes loop holes
Used and abused
While families are torn in two
Stolen childhoods that's true

So many children denied
The basic right, an education
Believe me this is the situation
In our nation

When will it stop
When will society care
Stop this cruelty
Does anyone really care

When will politicians
Stand up and take note
When will they choose to look
At all the abuse

Maybe one day
Someone will look
At such abuse of power
When money is not an ivory tower

When a child is more
Than money or power
When they are valued more
than scoring a point

All families ask
Is for someone to be taken to task
To see the corruption
We need a solution

Who will stand
Who will fight
Who will defend
Families rights

A FREE WILD CHILD THATS ME!!!

I see you my boy of wonder
Wild, free allowed to simply be
No to conformity
And societies perceived sense of normality

You question their reality
You dare to find your reality
While they try to crush your originality
Your reach out without partiality

Your smile melts the heart
Your tears destroy the heart
Your child like demeanour
Filled with innocent humour

If they took the time to know you
The real you
Not societies dim view
They would see the beauty within you

Your insatiable hunger
For knowledge you seek
Makes me wonder
When do you sleep

The insatiable hunger
To learn more
To be more
No one can put asunder

No one can dim the light
The fire that burns so bright
The illuminating light
From a wild and free child

Yes that's right
A child free to think
Free to learn,
Free to simply be

A child not born from conformity
A child taught to question
A child taught self expression
A child free to simply be

Self expression through clothes
Hair and so much more
To walk his own path
To determine his own path

The freedom to chose
The freedom to be
The freedom to explore
Who and all he can be

Mistakes will be made
Triumphs too that's for sure
But learn we will
On this journey so pure

Oh my boy of wonder
With your own unique power
The strength to simply be
All you can be

Embrace the true you
Let know one tell you
Your less or more
Or that they know you

Don't bow down
Don't be put down
You are you
Wild, free, special to me

Society will one day see
The children with inner strength
Born unique, determined and free
Will heal and change this world

Yes stay wild and free
Released from captivity
Known as conformity
Just simply be the best you can be

<u>SILENTLY TEAR DROPS FALL</u>

Tear drops fall
Silently upon the floor
No kind words
Or warm hugs

The stress and strain
The never ending pain.
The doubts
Comes about like a roundabout

Reassurance fails
When resistance prevails
The one in power
Sitting in their ivory tower

Every mistake
Every word said in haste
Every look of disdain
Causes the heart pain

The past remains
professionals use to their gain
Nothing can be let go
Because of their ego

Their need to be right
Is more
Than to do what is right
That's for sure

Doubt enters the heart
Questions what if?
Blinds the mind
And shreds the heart

The tears fall silently
Upon the pillow
No one to share
These troublesome cares

Masking the pain
Masking the strain
Hiding their disdain
It's oh so plain

If the heart could release
The past memories
The parenting abyss
The poison of gossip

We fight to do what's right
But is the fight worth it
Or do we loose sight
Of the target

The target for us support
Theirs a budget of sorts
Families destroyed
In secret courts

Who has the power
The money and resources
The local authorities
Of course

Who will suffer
Who will loose
The children that's who
Families torn in two.

Alone parents cry
Wishing their children could fly
With support they could
Praying for miracles we do

Deny they will
It's against their will
Bully they will
Resist we will

The tears and doubts
That's what it's about
We shout and shout
Others believe nowt

This is the reality
Painful hostility
Depravity, irregularity
Failing children regularly

This is the local authority
Families reality
Seek support we try
While they turn a blind eye

When will the majority
See the reality
No support is the reality
Failing children, Reality

Stand together as one
Together stand tall
Fight for one and all
Our children the world.

Tears fall gently, silently
Parents alone
No one to call
To break the fall

Families stand tall
Be like a wall
Protect all
Stand your grand, That's All!!

School Visit Reflection

Conform conform
To the neurotypical norm,
Flood me
Reward me
That's simply not for me

The smells the sounds
The lights and walls
The floors
Overwhelm me what's more

The clothes you were
The carpets on the stairs
Perfume, aftershave
Oh no food smells not to crave

Reward me, placate me
Then withhold from me
Choices I am to make
I am not even eight

Reflect you say
Whats the right way to behave
Higher executive skills
Deficits are why we differ
So make good choices never

However,
Enable me,
Celebrate me
See me flower
See me grow in power

Don't flood me
Then reward me
Not punish or withhold from me
What's that going to do me
Of course traumatise me

Yes I will conform
Under such a structure
But did you ever wonder
If that give me true power

It's not a choice
Neurological difference
So conformity
By by your therapy
Will simply destroy me

If you cannot celebrate with me
And see the real me
Separate the behaviour
From me
Then why try to get to know me

To know me
Is to give me a voice
To know me
Is to empower me

To know me
Is to enable me
To know me
Celebrate with me

To make me conform
Will break me
To neurotypicalise me
Will traumatise me

To make me behave
Your crush me
To make me conform
You flood me

My neurology is not my choice
But you took away my voice
My unique mind
Will blow you away in time

You will not destroy me
You will not quite me
You will not placate me
You will not flood me

I am me
The best that I can be
So stop trying to normalise me
Stop trying conformity

I am me
Unique
I am me
Empowered I will be

I am me
My voice is strong
I am me
I will not be wronged

I am me
I celebrate me
I am me
Simply the best I can be

FRIENDS ARE A TREASURE

Friends are a treasure
Friends are for ever
They accept you as you are
Do not run Far

They stick with you during hard times
Celebrate the good times
Don't run away when things get hard
Or avoid the phone calls simply because

Cherish friends
Loneliness is hard
Isolation breaks the heart
Celebrate all to lift the heart

Cherish friends
Celebrate make amends
Don't walk away
Don't run away

Yes friends are a treasure
Nothing can measure
Be strong, be kind
Don't break the mind

Friends are a treasure
Priceless and forever
Times may be hard
But friends are assured

To stand firm and fast
By your side is a must
One day it may be them
Who you will stand by again

PAST PAIN BETWEEN US

I read a book today
To find another way
Love and compassion
The order of the day

As a mum tears run down
When truth became clear
Disconnection from past pain
Between us came

My beautiful child
To nurture you
To make you happy
To show you your value

That's my hearts desire
To not hurt you
To connect with you
Enjoying being with you

Make your life hard. Never
To see the world
Through bitter words. Never
But the treacherous heart is clever

My needs as a child unmet
My heart did disconnect
Fear of expressing need
Meant life was bitter not sweet

Opening up is hard
Bridling the tongue
Oh what a charade
But I didn't want to make you sad

My tears I shed tonight
As the words brought light
Expressing with words
My heart in knots

I want my words to connect
Our needs to meet
With mutual respect
Not to brow beat

Empathy not sympathy
Fully present not absent
What's alive in us
Let's focus on that

I love you, I love you
Please remember that
When my human frailty
Runs amuck I'll get unstuck

I will take my time
It's yours and mine
To hear you
Be there for you

I will love you
Unconditionally
Compassionately
Til the end of time.

CONCEDED

Today the email came
Bitter sweet all the same
Placement agreed
They claimed

Two years down the line
Family decline
Financial decline
Trying to make me toe the line

Professional assault
Threats All covert
Family laws broke
Send regulations a joke

I screamed with glee
Then was hit with reality
The battle not over
As they tried to get one over

Visit your home
Discuss amendments
They wrote
What a joke

Working document
Needs and provision
Tribunal agreement
That's what I envision

No working document
No agreement
On needs and provision
Still they try division

Advocate advocate
They try to obliterate
Their objective
Divide and separate

No parental involvement
Or consent
Discussions prevalent
My views absent

My answer
Liaise with advocate
Apologies they sent
But liaise they did not yet

EHC document
A joke at present
As Local Authorities
Take further liberties

Families taken to hell
Broken down as well
Money the priority
The child the minority

Concede you say
But what a price to pay
Families laid bare
Vulnerable and scared

Concede you say
Telling me what to do
No tribunal for you
Not what I say, at the end of the day

Illegally you act
That's the fact
Let's remember that
No forgiveness that's what

Destroying my family
Was part of the plan
To safe money if you can
You'll do it, you plan

OBSESSION OR ISOLATION ?

Sometimes when coming home,
We reflect on what's been said and done,
We are all alone,
Isolated because we are not societies norm

Criticise we tend to be
Because we won't let things be
We speak to much, say to much
About topics that feel safe to us

Simple chit chat for what it's worth
Isn't comfortable for us
Safe subject what is that
Can get us into trouble that's what

We talk about what we know
Professionals are supposed to be in the know
But life experience that's all we know
But focusing on it is the final blow

Life experience can create so much pain
We try and prevent history repeat the same
They don't understand ,When we make a stand
Instead our words are used as weapons to blame,

When isolated at home and out and about
You lose topics to talk about
When fighting your children's corner
It looks obsessive to the onlooker

When will your realise
how the past affects our hearts
To watch our loved ones,
Go down the same path

Society communicates with such disdain
What they believe we hope to gain
The professionals also join in
They don't understand the pain

Growing up isolated and alone
The bullying, lack of support
All the dreams we had to abort
Still now an adult we stand alone

School life too painful to report
Bullying the reality of our life
Now we fight for support
Our children deserve a better life

Rather than ask the reality of our drive
Professionals and others alike
Accuse and threaten that's what they are like
All we want is our children to thrive

So support groups what do we focus on,
What health professionals see as obsession
Children's behaviours, challenges, and isolation
So then they brow beat us into submission

Ask us what we really want to talk about
But no longer share our shout about
The reason is when we share what we need
It's used as a weapon because of your greed

Isolation in its many forms
Is painful because we are unable to conform
We talk what we know about
Put our foot in it there is no doubt

Take a step back
And ask what is it all about
A driven need to prevent history
Repeating itself can you imagine that

Anxiety in social situations
The ability to mask
Can create so many misgivings
Finding solutions a massive task

Look for solutions to support
Would be a Start
Preventing isolation in communities
Also a start

Be willing to explore
Be willing to listen even more
give credence to our fears
Don't increase them by listening to peers

Take the time to peel back the layers
Built up over many many years
Text books are okay but not the reality
Our walls have been built protecting our sanity

What do you know about me
have you asked about my reality
Have you given me the safe space
To hear the parents interests

I am more than autistic
More than a parent
More than what I portray
But you've not given me the safety

We talk about what we think is right
What's simply consuming our hearts and minds
For our children we seek a better life with all our might
You do not delve deep negative opinions you keep

Obsession or super driven
Truth or opinion
Stereotyping and isolation
My reality or your perception

DANCE OF PRE-TENSE

Little boy off to ballet school goes
Full of hope dreams no woes
Mum is so happy
Because he is so happy

Goes to collect
Oh but what is this
A teacher full of regrets
Opinions strange what is this

Oh mother before me
Your son today opinions gave
Strange ideas he did relay
So regrettably he cannot stay

Please elaborate won't you please
Well today the truth did tell
Santa is no fairy tail
Santa is real he did tell

So mother before me this I say
Your opinion and teaching
Well what can is say
Not here in my class is what I say

Sarcasm from my mouth does flow
Dear mother this is what I propose
Your son of five
Can go into the class of 11-13s right

Mother turns to her boy
feels the boys woe
Anxiety begins to flow
Wail he does plain no

Mum walks away with boy in tow
Tears begin to flow
Heartbreak to follow
Her sons hopes no more

To a cafe they go,
Mum tries to stem the flow
As they enter the cafe
Oh no more sorrow

Another Mum sits and discusses
Child possible spectrum be
A little on the spectrum aren't we all
Believe me it's far from so

On the spectrum a little or more
Lonely isolation such a contradiction
Oh and what's more
Condemned and judged

No compassion for us
Children ousted
Clubs, groups School too
We are on a bit on the spectrum
Though don't think so

Look at the child sat at my side
Rejected again ,For simply being him
More than a bit on the spectrum
Reality is a little on is far from

If only you knew the truth
The rejections, all the blows
The gossip that simply flows
And so much pain caused

A statement so often said
Thoughtless hurtful words
That they never regret
But that we never forget

Walk in my shoes
Walk in my sons shoes
Live our lives
Then you will see

We are not all a little on the spectrum
We feel the pain
Never quite fitting in
Rejected over and over again

He told the truth
Now confused it's too much
What a painful blow
Knocking a child so low

Thought Christmas was a time for joy
Time for peace and love to bestow
But no my boy hurt once more
So adults could perpetuate their lies even more

Now a little boy of five
Wants to hide
No longer to dance
Crushed by your pretence

SNOW FALL JOY

Simply Joy
Snow fall
Out we go
Simple pure joy

Such a rush
Shoes not a must
I just need the snow
To fall upon me you know

So out he goes
So full of joy
The snow falling
A time for frolicking

Up and down he goes
Excitement and squeals
All because the snow falls
Gently upon his brow

In and out he runs
Snow upon his hands
Patterns he shows me
His passion overflowing

See a simple joy
From a snow flake
From snow fall
He is having a ball

My little boy
So wild and free
Conformity oh no
Be you be more

Don't let society crush
Your simple beauty
Your innocence
Your tenacity

Be wild and free
Be unique
Daily find simple joy
Do all that you enjoy

I love you my amazing son
Your determination, your passion
Your analytical and creative mind
It pure gentle and mild

You will change the world
my little rainbow child
Stand firm bold and wild
Free to simply be

GOSSIP RIVER

Gossip is like a ruined river
Flowing everywhere
A Destructive life force
Fuelled by hate of course

Here's the scenario
Let's see where this river flows
Can we see the connections
I believe so

A little boy to nursery goes
Punished severely
Step in we did they say
More than once a day

Why you may ask
For blowing bubbles into a glass
For climbing a slide The wrong way
Teddy bears taken away

Sensory seeking processing deficits
Meant they punished him
For simply being him
Because in societies rule he did not fit in

Then the mum to a home educating group goes
Hopes he will finally be understood of course
Oh no you see connections she did not see
Nursery staff and organisers
Best friends are we

Again the child is misunderstood
Treating as naughty
Beguiled, ostracised and treated harshly
Gossip possibly, let us see? Maybe!

The little boy could not breathe
Run out he did
So Lifted your hand behind him
As he rushed out pretend to hit him

The child on the floor
Your cane by his face what's more
Hit the Lego with the cane
Towards his face once again

Oh no no more
Mum a volcano
Meltdown city
Oh how dare you

Mum and child do leave
Disheartened to say the least
Alone, judged, criticised
All mums fault they decide

Treating the little boy as naughty
Saying blaming mums parenting
What do you say
Gossip leads the way

Then again we see the flow
The comments did flow
Appropriate educational setting
Inappropriate age related education

They could not see
Their minds blinded by a twisted reality
By others truths and opinions unfortunately
the gossip river flows unnaturally

Carry on we do alone
The little boy support
Finally to come
The battle won

The flow of gossip
Is cruel and destructive
Driven by others perceptions
The child becomes the victim

From adults preconceived misconceptions
False accusations and retaliations
Lack of understanding of the autistic spectrum
From their lips the destructive gossip slips

Please in future
Think before the words slip
Over the damn of pursed lips
Of the potential pain and turmoil

The gossip river overflowing
Permeates all boundaries
Of all sensibilities
Disabling, isolating

No- one says sorry for the pain caused
No-one admits they were wrong of course
No two wrongs make a right
I no longer want to fight

Too much joy taken away
As the destructive river flows again
Tears they flow readily
As others words slip thoughtlessly

Tired and exhausted
Hearts crushed and busted
The river named Gossip
Destroys families it's so toxic

Thanks to the friends
Who took the time
To understand
Stemming the bitter flow
Of river gossip flow

Thanks to the friends
Who stood up tall
Helped build a wall
Positive loving and strong

Thanks to the friends
Who did believe
In the child's potential
along with the family

Thanks to the friends
Who saw so much more
Than the hurtful gossip flow
And stood tall

Took the time to get to know
That beautiful little boy
The river gossip is not your guide
Your not blind you know you own mind

CHRISTMAS

A child walks by
Tears in his eyes
Overwhelmed
By the Christmas lights

Lashing out
Shout and scream
To others plain naughty
For him just pain

A stranger walks by
Sees the child
Exclaims he is naughty
Santa won't be calling tonight

A parent walks by
Tears in her eyes
Guilt and shame, blame
For the toys she can't buy

A parent walks by
Overwhelmed at heart
Can't explain
The pain again not tonight

Prioritise tonight
Food, toys, bills
It's such a fight
To do what's right

A stranger walks by
Condemnation in the eye
As parent says to child
Sorry I can't buy that tonight

This season
Has no rhyme or reason
For further debt
Stress and heartbreak

Santa is mean the child explains
Why parent asks ,Give me your reason
Because toys are not given
To all children this season

Explain my dear
Collection toy boxes for children
Not getting this season
Means he not given to some
It's beyond all reason

Son says to mum
Why is that mum mean
Taking her sons present
That Santa is leaving

To that child thought to be naughty
Imagine the reinforced reality
When the present desired
Santa has brought nought

Not because he is naughty
But parent just didn't have the money
Imagine the guilt and shame
The pain because of internal blame

A child's worth is not defined
By gifts and presents at this time
The parents worth is not defined
By the presents bought at this time

Words cut like a knife
Break the heart and the mind
Leave judgements behind
Let our words be gentle and kind

Pause for a moment
Think of blessings we have
What's truly important
Is the family we have

Family discuss the reason
For this season
Our family together
Not alone, or cold we are together

Simple blessings
A home, a bed,
Food for our belly
Heating, clothing,
Some of many

Not living in a war zone
A hostel or refuge
Not living in fear
Though we may shed a tear

What's important
Family and friends
But remember those
Who will be so alone

Though our times are hard
Many others harder times face
No home, no friends,
Shown no warmth or grace.

Comparisons can create much pain
But also insight
Blessings of love and light
To all those in this dark night

Dark times ahead

Many truly will face
It's not about saving face
Let's look further ahead

Let's be brave
Community come join together
Build each other up
Not tear down

Compassion, love and joy
Is better than any toy
Community spirit
Will bring better benefits

Together we stand divided we fall
Pride before many a fall
Hold your head and heart up high
Let you community light shine bright

2017

Printed by Amazon Italia Logistica S.r.l.
Torrazza Piemonte (TO), Italy

12284017R00021